CONCRETE POETRY

Paul Bernard

Cabinet of Concrete Poetry, MAMCO Geneva

Cabinet of Concrete Poetry, MAMCO Geneva (Franz Mon's exhibition)

Cabinet of Concrete Poetry, MAMCO Geneva (Ruth Wolf-Rehfeldt's exhibition)

TABLE OF CONTENTS

16

INTRODUCTION

Paul Bernard

Concrete Poetry is an artistic and literary movement, which emerged on the international scene during the 1950s. From Europe to Brazil, North America and Japan, a network of poets and artists have appropriated and reused the linguistic experiments of the Dadaists, Futurists and Lettrists, as well as Apollinaire's calligrams, Mallarmé's "A Throw of the Dice will Never Abolish Chance" and Ezra Pound's "The Cantos," to compose visual poems where words, morphemes, and letters become a material in themselves. In his 1953 *Manifesto for Concrete Poetry*, the Swedish artist Öyvind Fahlström wrote: "Poetry can be … created as structure. Not only as structure emphasizing the expression of idea content, but also as concrete structure." By working on the typography's plasticity and the poem's formatting, Eugen Gomringer's reductionism, Seiichi Niikuni's repetitions, Jiri Valoch's fragmentations, and herman de vries' naturalist compositions jeopardized the meaning of language. These raw forms triggered this "tension of things-words in space-time," to quote Augusto de Campo's definition, where what the poem *says* has as much value as what it *shows*.

A permanent space at MAMCO is devoted to the presentation of this unique genre, at the crossroads of literature and visual arts. Inaugurated in 2017, the Cabinet of Concrete Poetry enjoys its own space and program within the museum. It started with a large deposit of works on paper from the Zona Archives. The collection, curated by Italian artist Maurizio Nannucci together with German art historian Gabriele Detterer, consists of over 30,000 documents on avant-garde art practices, including artists' books, small presses, audio works, and one of the world's largest collections of Concrete Poetry. Between 2017 and 2020, a series of exhibitions entitled *Around Concrete Poetry* and *About Concrete Poetry* explored this collection, giving an insight into the diversity of practices and the international dimension of the movement. These first projects also sought to highlight Concrete Poetry's endeavour to challenge—like all avant-garde practices—its own orthodoxy and its affinities with other movements such as Conceptual art and Fluxus.

In 2018, the Cabinet acquired specially designed furniture by Juliette Roduit. Two map cabinets, mounted on wheels and topped with display cases, provide both display and storage space for the entire collection. Being mobile, the cabinet may travel on certain occasions. Besides, its simplicity and practicality parallel the works' accessibility and lightness. Audio equipment also offers the sonic dimension to the viewers, revealing the tenuous connections between Concrete Poetry and sound poetry.

A first monographic exhibition was organized in 2020 with Franz Mon. In the same year, the cabinet moved to the ground floor to join in the *John Giorno Poetry's Day* by hosting an evening of readings with the Centre d'Art Contemporain de Genève. In 2021, the cabinet finally settled on the third floor, in "L'Appartement," reminding us of the bridges that may have existed between Concrete Poetry and Conceptual art. This relocation opened with an exhibition of works on paper by Ruth Wolf-Rehfeldt and emphasized another dimension of Concrete Poetry: its international outreach via Mail art, which circumvented communist regimes' censorship.

At the end of 2020, the Zona Archives were handed over to Maurizio Nannucci. MAMCO then acquired an important collection from the publisher and gallery owner Steven Leiber (1957–2012). When he opened his gallery in San Francisco in 1981, he quickly recognized the significance of the ephemera and documentation related to Fluxus, Conceptual art, Beat culture and Concrete Poetry, and began to specialize in these works on paper, which had hitherto been on the margins of art history. His graphic design skills and professionalism have earned him international reputation. In 2001, he was invited to curate a major exhibition dedicated to these mediums (*Extra Art: A survey of Artist's Ephemera from 1960–99*, Wattis Institute, San Francisco).

The Leiber collection of Concrete Poetry acquired by the MAMCO comprises 400 items featuring ephemera, posters, journals, anthologies as well as collections' inventories. Leiber's expertise led him to inventory a few prestigious collections, including Marvin and Ruth Sackner's, the largest in the world. Due to their meticulousness and particular layout, these numbered and signed inventories became valuable in themselves. Around 100 works (mainly books and artists' editions) from the MAMCO collection have been added to the Leiber collection. In 2022, the Cabinet of Concrete Poetry will bring together almost 500 items and further expand its collection. Each of its exhibitions entails acquisitions, among other things.

2

ABOUT CONCRETE POETRY

Maurizio Nannucci interviewed by Paul Bernard

PB   The Cabinet of Concrete Poetry which we have set up at the MAMCO with you and Gabriele Detterer presents a part of the Zona Archives collection in Florence. Could you give us some details about this organization?

MN   Zona Archives is a "vice" and one of the passions in my life! It is a project that has developed alongside my own work and research. I started to bring together documents about the experimental practices that were close to me (Concrete Poetry, electronic music, artists' books and records, small presses, the ephemeral scene, etc.), since the second half of the 1960s. Over time, and thanks to the activities of Zona, an associative space based in Florence from 1974 to 1985, a large archive has been built up, consisting of tens of thousands of documents, which I often present in museums and libraries. In particular when it comes to concrete poetry, because this is the first phenomenon that I became involved in, and the first time that my work became caught up in an international context.

PB   Can you explain what Concrete Poetry is?

MN   Concrete Poetry rose to prominence at the end of the 1950s, as one of the most radical artistic movements of the second half of the 20th century. Becoming immediately international, this movement brought together authors and artists coming from various disciplines. Its most characteristic contribution was the elaboration of texts/images based on new syntaxes, which could for example be geometrical or spatial. Its productions exalted the semantic and aesthetic plasticity of words by using their typographical elements, while respecting their threefold function of being verbal, visual, and phonetic. Concrete Poetry opened up new perspectives for "verbal art", as an experimental practice. It transcended the literary categories of its originals, so as to evolve in direct contact with avant-garde practices, while occasionally anticipating them, at once in music, architecture and design.

PB How did you organize your choices from this archive?

MN The material and documents which we are presenting in the Cabinet, for which I wanted specific furniture to be produced, tell the story of a journey, or shift from the representation of images to texts. I think that, of all the experiments of the mid-1950s, Concrete Poetry was a space that was crossed over by many things that happened later in the world of art—ranging from Fluxus to Conceptual or Minimal art.

PB Could it be said that Concrete Poetry provides the possibility for people coming from the worlds of literature and the visual arts to meet up?

MN There is basically this twofold nature, even if I think that the most interesting aspect was that the artists felt the need to look for new routes, and new horizons from which they could develop their own investigations. If we look at the books or works on display, we can understand that there are parallel interests, but also real differences. The practices of Brazilian poets such as Augusto and Haroldo de Campos or Décio Pignatari differ from the approaches of Italian poets and artists like me or Arrigo Lora Totino, or else Austrians like Ernst Jandl, Gerhard Rühm and Heinz Gappmayr, or representatives from America, such as Emmett Williams and Robert Lax, France, like Henry Chopin and Pierre and Ilse Garnier, Britain, with Ian Hamilton Finlay and John Furnival, or Germany with Ferdinand Kriwet and Franz Mon. With the latter, there emerged an importance for the investigations inspired by the thought of Max Bense and the structural theory of language, without forgetting some of Marshall McLuhan's postulates, such as "The Medium Is the Message."
So we also have to talk a little about the medium, in the sense that there is always a sort of ambiguity between the work and the document when it comes to concrete poetry. Poets tend to publish, because they like print, while artists remain marked by

their initial ideas. Concrete Poetry merges these two attitudes. What is more, we shouldn't forget the influence of graphic arts and typography, or else the development of a modern language that favoured lowercase letters and Helvetica, with a taste for the material nature of the result, as well as its haptic, or even three-dimensional nature.

PB   This also leads into being able to see the means of production from this era: serigraphy, the typewriter, verifax, letraset, and so on.

MN   The means of reproduction and information from that time cannot be compared to those of our digital age, but they did provide for an individual production with a quick and cheap distribution. Concrete Poetry led to a huge production of self-publications which were distributed worldwide. There were the Japanese artists Seiichi Niikuni and Kitasono Katue with the reviews *Vou* and *Asa*, while all of Europe was concerned, from Spain to Sweden, taking in Switzerland, with publications by Eugen Gomringer and Dieter Roth, and the Eastern bloc with Jiří Kolář and Jiří Valoch. The first manifesto of Concrete Poetry (1953) was produced by Öyvind Fahlström who claimed its paternity, while Eugen Gomringer described his investigations and the de Campos brothers in Brazil published *Noigandres*, their review of Concrete Poetry… All of this, and even more, is there to seek out and discover, while browsing through our Cabinet of Concrete Poetry.

futura 3   ir

max bense

tallose berge

o
rio
roi
oro
orior
orion
rionoir
ronronron

28

NOTES ||||||||||
ON ARTISTS

Paul Bernard
Thierry Davila

JULIEN BLAINE

Julien Blaine, born Christian Poitevin in 1942, has been a prominent figure in the poetry scene since the early 1960s (he founded his first journal, *Les Carnets de l'Octéor*, when he was 20). Polymorphous cultural actor and prolific poet, performer, creator, coordinator of journals and festivals, and politically committed, Blaine combines Action Poetry (he is one of its initiators), with elementary poetry and Mail art. Clearly, an irrepressible desire to transcend the poem's classical forms and formats drive his work. This "poésie à outrance" [outrageous poetry, in the sense of ultra-poetry, transgressing limits], to quote the title of an impressive monograph devoted to his work, places experimentation as the key motivation for a critical endeavour that also aims to keep the sign and the language alive.

In the 1960s, Blaine created and edited several journals, including *Robho* with Jean Clay, which featured six issues between June 1967 and the very beginning of 1971. This particularly remarkable publication, notably for its interest in non-European art and emerging forms (Franz Erhard Walther was interviewed by Yve-Alain Bois), was also a tool for exploring the "poetry outside the book," as described in a final unsigned editorial. This willingness to leave book's medium is most visible in the journal *Approches* fourth issue, published in 1969, founded by Julien Blaine and Jean-François Bory in 1965 (MAMCO acquired numbers 1 and 2). Blaine designed the cover and inserted as a booklet, his poem "Dernière tentative de l'individu" [Last attempt of the individual], subtitled "English – Poem", a calendar of the years 1968 and 1969 converted into a fold-out leporello. A wide black band runs through the length of the poem, with holes in the last pages to be unfolded. Once spread out, the leporello physically leaves the journal's space, thereby symbolizing the departure from the traditional poetry's frameworks, central to Blaine's work—and one of Concrete Poetry's mainsprings.

Thus, in *W M Quinzième*, no. 7 of the *Carnets de l'Octéor* published in 1966, Blaine offered a final poem at the end of the publication that is both visible and invisible—"Attansion !"—for the readers to complete as they wish. Again, poetry reached elsewhere: if it can be made by everyone, according to Lautréamont's adage, Blaine gave everyone the opportunity to achieve this poem's democratization by turning it, even as an edited object, into an open work. *The Petit précis d'érotomanie (fugue)* [A brief handbook of erotomania], published in 1969, is another example of poetic action: its handling being reserved for men—in one reading direction—and for women—in another. The optical and haptic object is therefore to be contemplated and activated. In this expansion of the poem's domain, Blaine perceived letters and words as some built bridges (*Les ponts sont des mots étirés* [Bridges are stretched words], 1967, a leporello whose expansive form parallels the book's subject). It also led him to experiment with poetic lability: in *Breuvage épandu* [Spread Beverage] (1967), consisting of a set of four black-and-white photographs, the alphabet's letters contained in a glass, are poured onto a table, making poetry an infinitely deterritorializable language flow.

Julien Blaine, *Dernière tentative de l'individu*, 1968

JEAN-|||||||||||
FRANCOIS
BORY||||||||||||

Born in Paris in 1938, Jean-François Bory's work lies at the crossroads of poetry and the visual arts, as does his accomplice Julien Blaine with whom he founded the journal *Approches* in 1965 (Bory was in fact the only "editor in charge"), a "research journal" of only four issues between 1966 and 1969. A complete editorial structure whereby Bory published his own work but also Blaine's and Jochen Gerz's. Bory's books *Plein signe* [Full Sign], *whispering* and *[BÊCHE]* [SPADE], published by *Approches*, provide striking evidence of graphic space exploration using signs (dots, ideograms, formulas in English) conceived as visual tools in themselves, where the page acts as a site for appearance and circulation. The last two publications consist of handmade books printed with ink stamps in limited editions. After *Approches*, Bory founded the journal *L'Humidité* (1970–1978, 25 issues), he was its main coordinator and contributor, taking on pseudonyms such as Janusz Chodorowicz, Georges Unglik or Léonardo Nunez. Issue no. 18 (October 1973) is entirely devoted to his work, featuring essays by Giovanni Lista and Pierre Bourgeade, discussing his relation to the book as an object, which is also an important part of his connection to the sign and its materiality. Bourgeade offered the following description: "Jean-François Bory, most of the time, crafts his books using scissors and glue. According to

Jean-François Bory, *Logorinth IV*, n.d.

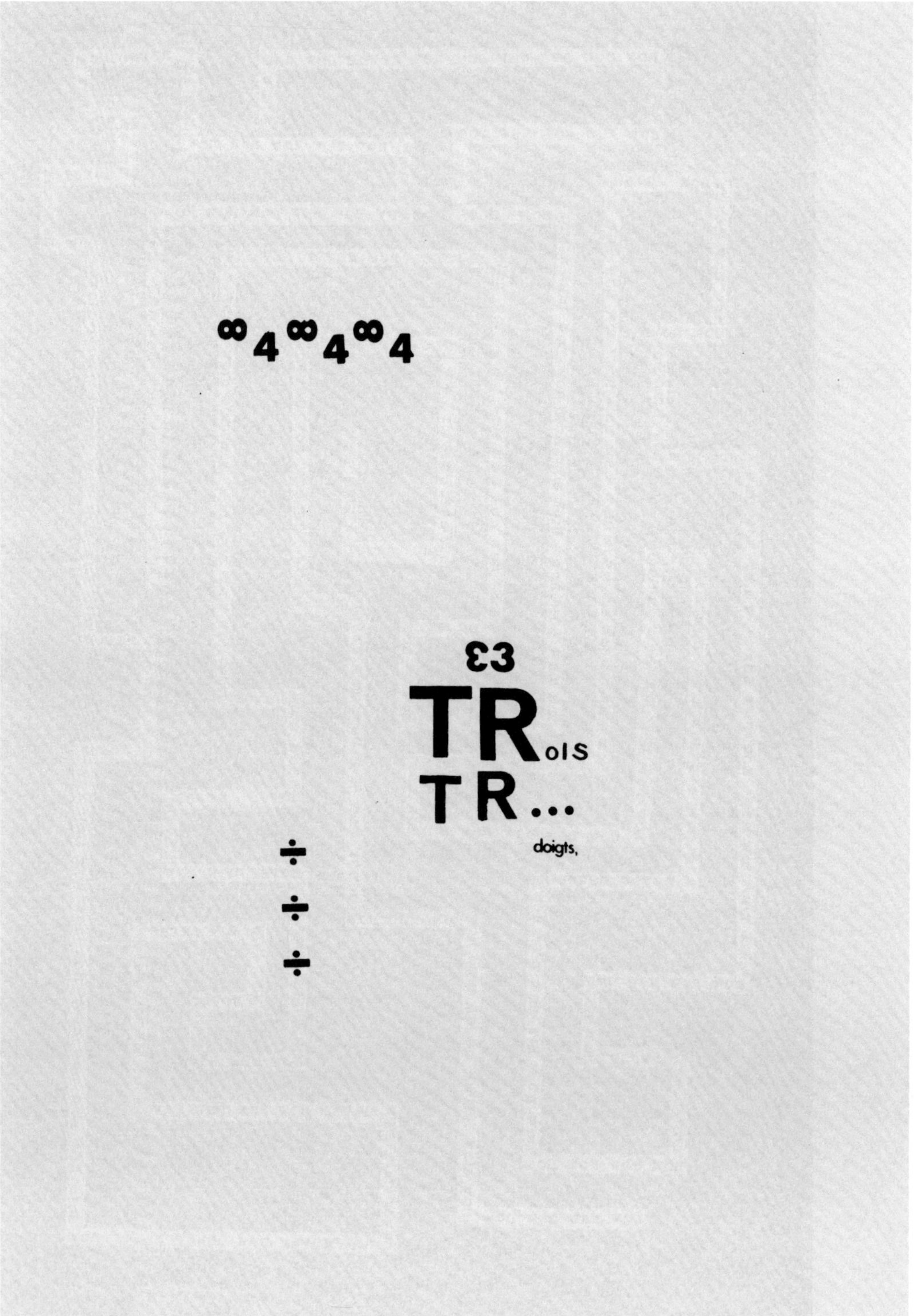

∞4 ∞4 ∞4

ε3
TRoIS
TR...
doigts,

÷
÷
÷

Jean-François Bory, *Arithmetic Text 4*, 1966

him, the book's material does not lie in what the mind conveys through the book [...] but in the book itself, in what makes it a book and nothing else: paper, ink, thread, glue, cardboard. [...] This is no longer 'Degree Zero': it is the Writing Third Degree. Writing is not only materialism, but—finally! Materiality."

In 1968, in New York, Bory published one of the very first anthologies collating international visual poetry and became a member of a vast artists and poets' international network exploring a spatialized poetry partly inspired by Concrete Poetry. During this period, he himself published *Height Texts + One* (the initial H referred to the H-bomb) for Gallery Number Ten in London, where letters, words, sentences, and cut-out black-and-white photographs are combined into expansive typography (his "Typoèmes" were exhibited in that same city in 1967). Figurative motifs also inhabit his visual poetry: in *Post-Scriptum*, published by Éric Losfeld in September 1970, cut-out photographs (notably of naked women and classical painting masterpieces) are mixed with cut-out letters, creating a connection between naming and representation. Even the number itself is poetized: printed in letterpress as 18 flyers slipped into an envelope, *Arithmetic Texts* (1967) placed the number at the centre of the page's visual exploration, extending the author's "typographic nourishment" (Nathalie Quintane) and his poetry's visualized spatiality.

BOB ||||||||||
COBBING|

Bob Cobbing (1920–2002), first known as the editor and publisher of *Writers Forum Poets*, was a leading figure in British avant-garde poetry. He notably managed *Better Books*, an essential venue for many of the artistic and literary happenings of the 1960s London Underground.

After the war, Cobbing began to work on monotypes using the typewriter's graphic possibilities, repeatedly typing the same piece of poetry on the page until its complete illegibility. In the process, he experimented with various visual effects, textures, and meanings. From 1954 onwards, Cobbing performed his poetry and became a major international sound poetry protagonist.

On the connections between Concrete Poetry and sound poetry, Cobbing explained: "Concrete Poetry is for me a return to an emphasis on the physical substance of language—the sign made by the voice, and the symbol for that sign made on paper or in other material and visible form. Leonardo da Vinci asked the poet to give him something he might see and touch and not just something he could hear. Sound poetry seems to me to be achieving this aim. Partly it is a recapturing of a more primitive form of language, before communication by expressive sounds became stereotyped into words, when the voice was richer in vibrations, more mightily physical."

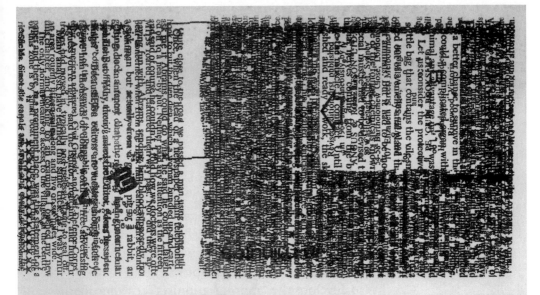

Bob Cobbing, *typestract*, 1965

NATALIE CZECH

Works by Natalie Czech (*1976) stand at the confluence of Concrete Poetry and "appropriationist" photography: movements that question the relationship between text and image. Czech applies the concrete poets' spatialization of text, and its inference of the equivalence between what a poem tells and shows, between the legible and the visible.

Czech also develops the "appropriationists" critique of originality, for which she substitutes "intertextuality," a concept that invites the viewer to consider every text as a fabric of quotations, in Roland Barthes's words. Czech's exclusively photographic work examines existing "textual fabrics" to reveal layers of meaning and poetry, in a play of unexpected connections, as in her *Hidden Poems*—a variety of reconfigured source materials in which the artist uses a pen or highlighter to reveal poems by E.E. Cummings, Jack Kerouac, Robert Lax, or Frank O'Hara. The original text is found to be "captioned" by this poetic revelation, while the second text acquires a new layout.

The Poet's question series takes and isolates questions from the poems of writers such as Lev Rubinstein, Robert Grenier, or Charles Bernstein as its starting point. The letters that make up these questions constitute a "stock," like the letters of a Scrabble, which the artist will seek in the objects of her daily life. One photograph reveals the question *Do hearts break if you don't touch them?* (from the poet Charles Bernstein) on an audio tape by the band Imperial Bedroom. The question is written in magnetic tape, as if the audio support itself was reproducing the text.

Natalie Czech, *A Poet's Question by Charles Bernstein (Cassette/Loved Ones)*
(Do hearts break if you don't touch them aabcdeefhhhikmnoooorrsttttuy), 2018

Natalie Czech, *A Poem by Repetition by Larry Eigner*, 2021

From music to text, and from poetry to photography, the self-referentiality is both intertextual and "inter-medial." If we look more closely at the tape, we see that each of the words used to write the question has been erased. With the exception of three words that form a troubling response: "Loved ones beat."

AUGUSTO DE CAMPOS AND THE NOIGANDRES GROUP

At the end of the 1940s, as São Paulo underwent an accelerated modernization, the brothers Augusto (*1931) and Haroldo de Campos (1923–2003) met Décio Pignatari (1927–2012) at the Law School. They shared an interest in poetry, soon started translating for newspapers and published their first books. In 1952, they launched *Noigandres*, an anthology magazine. Behind this enigmatic title, borrowed from Ezra Pound, the group embarked on a poetic journey that aimed to distance itself from the "post-war lyrical jargon: vegetative and reactionary," as Pignatari put it. They became involved with the artists of Grupo Ruptura (including Waldemar Cordeiro, Geraldo de Barros, Luiz Sacilotto, Lothar Charroux and Kazmer Féjer) and performed the first typographic and spatial experiments within their magazine. Between 1954 and 1956, Pignatari travelled to Europe where he met Pierre Boulez, John Cage, Karlheinz Stockhausen, and Eugen Gomringer in Ulm, then secretary to Max Bill. These meetings marked the

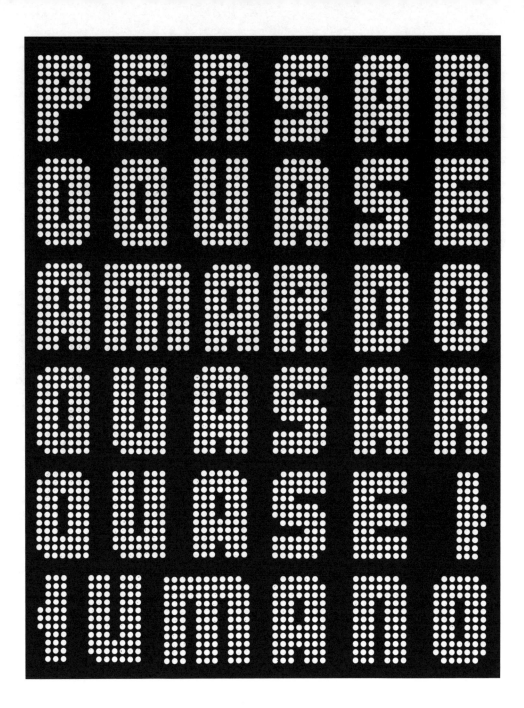

Augusto de Campos, *Quasar*, 1977

Augusto de Campos, Julio Plaza, *Caixa Preta*, 1975

beginning of an international poetic emulation. On Pignatari's return, the three poets began to theorize Concrete Poetry until the drafting of the "Pilot Plan for Concrete Poetry" published in 1958 in *Noigandres*, issue 4. Drawing on the poetry of Apollinaire, Mallarmé, Pound, and the Brazilians Oswald de Andrade and João Cabral de Melo Neto, they claimed a Concrete Poetry of "being aware of graphic space as structural agent." and insisted on the importance of the ideogram. "Concrete poem is an object in and by itself, not an interpreter of exterior objects and/or more or less subjective feelings," they stated, before concluding: "Concrete Poetry: total responsibility before language. Thorough realism. Against a poetry of expression, subjective and hedonistic. To create precise problems and to solve them in terms of sensible language. A general art of the word. The poem-product: useful object." The fifth and final issue of *Noigandres* was issued in 1962. The three poets then teamed up with other Brazilian artists and became the Invenção group, whose homonymous magazine, published between 1962 and 1967, featured the work of other poets including Max Bense, Ian Hamilton Finlay, and Pierre Garnier.

Within this Brazilian group, Augusto de Campos stands out notably for his connection with music. His first works, the *poeta-menos* (1953), alternate typographies of various colors, each representing a distinct voice scattered across the page. One of them was later translated into music by Caetano Veloso. In 1968, Augusto de Campos collaborated for the first time with the Spanish immigrant artist Julio Plaza (1937–2003). The *Poemóbiles* (1974) revisited some of de Campos's poems on three-dimensional cards.

The two artists worked together again in 1975 for the *Caixa Preta* (The Black Box), of which MAMCO owns a copy. It is a boxed set consisting of a few works on cardboard, creating various spatial configurations for the "reader" to manipulate. Both an anthology and a miniature exhibition, the *Caixa Preta* features one of de Campos' most famous poems, *VIVA VAIA* (Hurrah/Hissing) (1968), dedicated to Caetano Veloso. At the end of the 1960s, de

Campos grew closer to tropicalist musicians [Tropicália], including the latter and Gilberto Gil. The poem *VIVA VAIA* paid tribute to the difficulties faced by Veloso, an avant-garde musician, particularly when he was booed at a music festival in 1968. Thus, the *Caixa Preta* includes a record of Veloso reading de Campos' poems. It also comprises *cidade/city/cité* (1963), a trilingual poem wherein a single line of words combines all the terms in Portuguese, English, and French ending in cidade, city, cité, from "atro-city," to "vora-city." This line of words, also oralized by the author in several interpretations, must be read in a single breath. It reflects both the order and chaos sprawling in modern cities. In addition, the *Caixa Preta* offers a version of *LIXO/LUXO* (1965), a poem wherein a play with typography reveals the word *LIXO* (rubbish) by "accumulating" the word *LUXO* (luxury). Written in 1964 shortly after the military coup in Brazil, this last poem adds a certain political resonance to the work.

IAN HAMILTON FINLAY

With nearly 200 works, the Scottish artist Ian Hamilton Finlay (1925–2006) is the most collected artist in MAMCO's collection of Concrete Poetry. Poet, sculptor, editor, landscape artist, and philosopher, Finlay is a discreet but essential figure in poetry and art from the 1960s onwards, as evidenced by his participation in the 1987 documenta and the numerous academic studies devoted to his work. However, he is nowadays a controversial figure for his ambiguous positions in the late 1980s. In fact, one of his works exhibited in 1987 at the Fondation Cartier in Paris aroused considerable uneasiness due to its reference to the Waffen-SS. Although the impugned sculpture did not glorify Nazism, it became the starting point for a smear campaign in France. This "Finlay affair," which has seen several twists and turns, continues today to oppose the artist's supporters and his detractors.

Finlay's contribution to poetry and art is nonetheless substantial. As Anne Moeglin-Delcroix wrote, "Finlay . . . is a precious example of an artist for whom Concrete Poetry is the unmistakable starting point of an oeuvre which will nevertheless not cease to reflect on and exceed itself." Finlay encountered the Swiss Eugen Gomringer and the editors of the Brazilian magazine *Noigandres* (Décio Pignatari and the brothers Haroldo and Augusto de Campos) in 1962. The following year, he abandoned the "academic" poetry of his early days to engage in the manufacture of small toys and write his first Concrete Poetry's volume, *Rapel, 10 fauve and suprematist poems*. This simultaneous development: toy making and the artist's involvement in Concrete

Ian Hamilton Finlay, *National Flag Series: Arcadia*, 1974

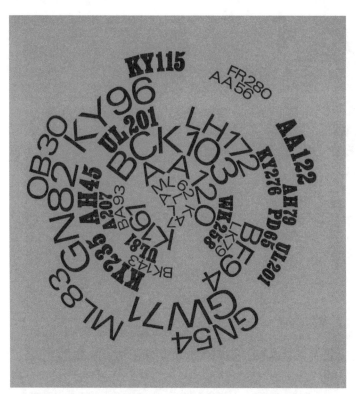

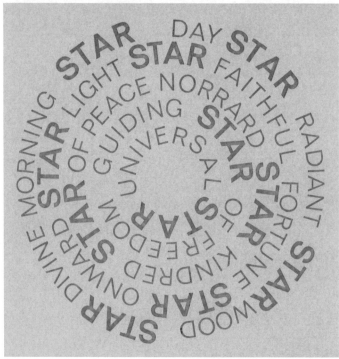

Ian Hamilton Finlay, *Sea-Poppy 1 (fishing boat letters and numbers)*, 1968
Ian Hamilton Finlay, *Sea-Poppy 2 (fishing boat names)*, 1968

Poetry was no coincidence. For Finlay, the two activities some-how corresponded: a Concrete poem is conceived as a language object and a game with letters. But already in this first volume, Finlay pointed out the aporias of Concrete Poetry through its desire to remain external to the world. Thereafter, he continued to work with very subtle means to break down its barriers, through his use of multiple media: postcards, micro-editions, books, posters, kites, sails, benches, posts, fences, walls, neon signs, dishes, and even fishing rod floats. This media and scales' heterogeneity is masterfully displayed in *Little Sparta*, his mag-num opus. Finlay moved to a small village south-west of Edinburgh in 1966 and started working on a vast garden where his poems and sculptures mingle with the trees, the flowers, and the pond: a direct confrontation of poetry with the world it is supposed to express. This "volume of poems that one does not leaf through" to paraphrase Francis Édeline, earned him world-wide fame and is still open to visitors today.

The works on paper acquired by the Cabinet of Concrete Poetry offer an insight into the artist's trajectory and its recur-ring themes. With a disconcerting economy of means, his poems connect the construction of words with those of the world. This is particularly evident in the one-word poems featured in *Air Letters* (1968), consisting of a disproportionately long title fol-lowed by a text of a single word or even a single letter, resem-bling the answer to a riddle. Elsewhere, Finlay played with the permutations or homophony of different words to produce unex-pectedly meaningful correspondences (*Canal Stripe 4, Wave or Wave Sheaf*).

The works on paper exhibit a few recurring patterns. First, we have the picturesque landscapes, the mills, and the sundials. Devoid of human presence, these pieces exude a certain neoclas-sicism. Arcadia, the mythical antique region with its lush and har-monious nature, was a source of inspiration. Finlay even drew a flag with skull and crossbones (*National Flag Series: Arcadia*, 1974), referring to Nicolas Poussin's famous Memento Mori, *Et in*

Ian Hamilton Finlay, *Earthship*, 1965

Arcadia ego (1628–1630), a paragon of classical art. The sea is another recurring theme, manifest in the sailing and fishing's motifs. Again, it is rendered through peaceful feelings, free of any storm or lyrical effusion. The permutations and repetitions allow us to see navigation as a "seam" of the sea (*sea ms*) and the ships as the setting for a cosmic confrontation with the stars (*star/steer*) or with the wind (*sails/waves*). The prevalent fishing activity is also understood as a parable of the poet's "capture of meaning", as analysed by Stephen Bann, Finlay's oeuvre main exegete.

MAMCO also houses several of Finlay's tributes to other painters and poets mostly made on postcards, yet, quite difficult to decipher. While expressing recognition, they also suggest a form of continuity and a two-fold tradition, both pictorial and poetic. In his pantheon we encounter the likes of Poussin, Watteau, Seurat, Kandinsky, Max Bill, Robert Lax, Jonathan Williams, and even the Pop art genre. These homages also gave Finlay the opportunity to work in a very humorous way, "in the style of," notably by twisting quotes. For instance, the tribute to Kahnweiler, who wrote an essay on Juan Gris, turned the subtitle of this book, "his life and work," into "his knife and fork," insisting on the "taste" of the Cubist painter's still lifes.

We might also mention *Ocean Stripe 5*, a pivotal work in Finlay's oeuvre, as it marked a significant departure from the Concrete Poetry's rigorism. The book consists of black and white photographs depicting fishing boats along with short statements about concrete and sound poetry. All the material is borrowed: the pictures came from the fishing magazine *Fishing News*, while the texts were taken from poets such as Ernst Jandl, Paul de Vree, and Kurt Schwitters. At first the quotations are closely connected to Concrete Poetry, then gradually detach themselves from it. It begins with "sound and concrete poetry substitutes the conventional and subjective type of poem with a universal and autonomous object" and ends with "it is impossible to explain the meaning of art; it is infinite." With this book, Finlay stated that he did not want to break with the Concrete poets, but rather further their research on more uncertain grounds. Offering a sense of metaphor for his future poetic endeavour, the Scotsman commented the book's last boat illustration: "A white vessel illuminated by the sun, sailing into a dark estuary."

JOHN ||||||||
FURN|VAL

Along with Dom Sylvester Houédard, John Furnival (1933–2020) was the main Concrete Poetry's protagonist in England. Graphic designer by profession, he defined himself as a drawer of landscapes, personages, and "wordscapes." He first developed a minimalist Concrete Poetry and eventually produced maximalist visual poetry. In 1964, together with Houédard and Edward Wright, he founded the publishing house *Openings*, specialized in Concrete Poetry's distribution. Besides poetry, performance and music were two very significant sources of his inspiration. In 1975, he brought together several artists and musicians to initiate the band *Satie's Faction*, in homage to Erik Satie, combining music, poetry, and performance.

His *wordscapes* were made by drawing letters, words, sentences, and long passages directly on paper, cardboard, or painted panels. Thus, words and letters appear as structural and compositional elements within texts, meant to be experienced as paintings or drawings, but also readable in fragments. Towers (the Tower of Babel in particular) and labyrinths are recurring motifs, as well as spiritual imagery and linguistic gymnastics.

Insofar as his works accumulated verbal and visual data to the extent of confusion, they belonged less to an orthodox definition of Concrete Poetry than to what Furnival himself labelled as "anti-concrete" poetry, requiring an "architectured reading".

John Furnival, *Untitled (BOOM!)*, n.d.

JOHN FURNIVAL - OPENINGS PRESS 1973 - MANHATTAN

John Furnival, *OPENINGS PRESS 1973 - MANHATTAN*, 1974

PIERRE & ILSE GARNIER

Pierre Garnier (1928–2014), a German teacher and translator of Nietzsche, wrote his first poems following the École de Rochefort, a poetic movement initiated in 1941 as a response to the "national poetry" championed by the Vichy regime and advocating individual expression. However, throughout the 1950s, he gradually distanced himself from this movement and developed a writing style based on verbal dislocation reminiscent of Ezra Pound. He met Henri Chopin in 1956 and Eugen Gomringer at the end of the 1950s, when he began his first visual poems. In 1962, together with his wife Ilse Garnier (1927–2020), he took over the magazine *Les Lettres* published by André Silvaire and exclusively focused on spatial, visual, concrete, and sound poetry. "To me, all these poems seemed related in terms of space, considered as the essential structural agent of poetry, hence the name of the journal of spatialism." In January 1963, issue 29, Pierre Garnier published his *Manifeste pour une poésie visuelle et phonique* [Manifesto for a visual and phonic poetry], spatialism's seminal text. This movement (unrelated to Lucio Fontana's) defended a conception of poetry where space forms its active element, able to influence the words' meaning. Poetry is therefore seen as an art of setting in space and required a liberation of the word, whose repressed or even forgotten potential must be revealed through its sound and visual material. The Garnier's wrote: "Free the words. Respect the words. Do not enslave them to sentences. Let them occupy their own space. They are not meant to describe, teach or tell: they are primarily meant to be. Words exist only in the wild. The sentence is the civilized state of words."

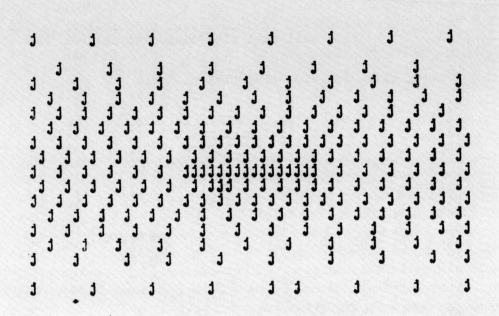

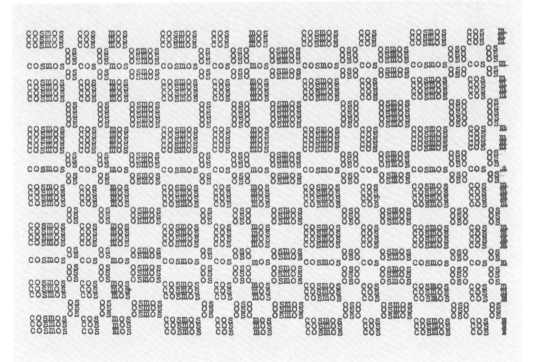

Pierre Garnier, "j" from the series *Prototypes, Textes pour une architecture*, 1966
Pierre Garnier, "cosmos" from the series *Prototypes, Textes pour une architecture*, 1966

Pierre Garnier, Seiichi Niikuni, "ciel" from the series *Poèmes franco-japonais*, 1967

This liberation also involved a sound dimension: Pierre Garnier started making his "Sonies" from 1963 onwards, where the breath is a driving and structuring element. As he wrote: "I freed the poetry from sentences, words, and articulations. I expanded it to the point of breath." These sound poems, recorded on a tape recorder, were radio broadcasted by Henri Chopin. The couple's research into the language's objectification led them to work on the "aesthetic information of words." In *Prototypes-Textes pour une architecture* [Prototypes-Texts for Architecture] (1965), the spatial dimension of poetic language can be experimented with functional industry manufactured objects to create a living, "habitable poetry." The Garniers thus showed a desire for an active participation of poetry within society. In 1964, Pierre Garnier introduced the *Poèmes mécaniques*, using the typewriter to imprint his body movements: "The mechanical poem (produced with the typewriter's letters) is a set of linguistic elements articulated to each other in such a way that the action of a force exerted on one of them may be transmitted to the others and counteract the poem's stasis."

In 1963 Garnier met the Japanese Concrete poet Seiichi Niikuni (1925–1977). From then on, both began to exchange texts composed collaboratively, the *Poèmes Franco-Japonais* (1967), mixing Latin alphabet and Japanese ideograms.

DOM ||||||||||||
SYLVESTER
HOUÉDARD|

Dom Sylvester Houédard (1924–1992), also known by the initial "dsh", was a Benedictine monk, theologian, and leading theorist of concrete and sound poetry in England. He was also noted for his spiritual theories, sharing, and working with the likes of Allen Ginsberg, Jack Kerouac, Ian Hamilton Finlay, and David Medalla.

Houédard's poetic approach was strongly influenced by a sense of spiritual quest. In 1964, he described Concrete Poetry: "from this very simple pure FORM comes something that affects the content the absence of the poets self in the poem—concrete is I-less". This desire for the absence of the self, manifested within the poem, came with the search for a form that no longer depended on words. To this end, he made particular use of the typewriter's possibilities, creating abstract typo-visual compositions where the letter itself was the primary material. His "typestracts," as he called them, are all typed on a portable *Olivetti lettera 22*. His abstract and uncluttered works suggest how the mechanical device's keys had become the instruments of a spiritual meditation.

Dom Sylvester Houédard's poetic research can indeed be likened to the Tantric and Buddhist practices that fascinated him. For Guy Brett, these *typestracts* "are of the same nature as mandalas and other cosmic diagrams." Houédard stated: "in the moments of making ... they step by step control me & pose ultimate questions of their own identity dependence destiny & independence."

Dom Sylvester Houédard, *...like contemplation...*, 1972

RICHARD ||||||||||
KOSTELANETZ|

Born in 1940 in New York, Richard Cory Kostelanetz is a prolific editor, artist, critic, teacher, poet, and author. After publishing texts in journals such as *Partisan Review*—where Clement Greenberg was a contributor—, *The Hudson Review*, but also *The New York Times Magazine*, he carried out a well-documented research work on the New York art scene (*SoHo: The Rise and Fall of an Artists' Colony*, 2003). His *Conversations with John Cage* remain an essential reference for anyone interested in the American composer's work.

Following a radical formalist approach in his poetry, he published *In the Beginning* in 1971, a thirty-page text where the alphabet is formed out of one or two letters' combinations. His visual poetry generally involves word assemblages on a page, especially using wordplays and alliterations, perhaps most visible in the books: *Visual Language* (1970), *Wordworks* (1993), *More Wordworks* (2006) (MAMCO acquired a copy of *Visual Language*). Kostelanetz creates graphic compositions devoid of color using letters and words as patterns. Triangles, lines, crosses, circles reveal linguistic or literary configurations: language essentially determined their visual composition, even if Kostelanetz may sometimes work with abstract geometrical forms (*I Articulations/Short Fictions*, 1974). In the Rimbaldian-titled booklet *Illuminations* (1977), handwritten in large font, the word "fissure" has been split in two in its middle: the form of the noun fully conveys its meaning. These are the kinds of games with letters, words, and aspects explored by Kostelanetz, who can also use numbers to invent

```
RADARADARADARADARADARADAR
ADARADARADARADARADARADARA
DARADARADARADARADARADARAD
ARADARADARADARADARADARADA
RADARADARADARADARADARADAR
ADARADARADARADARADARADARA
DARADARADARADARADARADARAD
ARADARADARADARADARADARADA
RADARADARADARADARADARADAR
ADARADARADARADARADARADARA
DARADARADARADARADARADARAD
ARADARADARADARADARADARADA
RADARADARADARADARADARADAR
ADARADARADARADARADARADARA
DARADARADARADARADARADARAD
ARADARADARADARADARADARADA
RADARADARADARADARADARADAR
ADARADARADARADARADARADARA
DARADARADARADARADARADARAD
ARADARADARADARADARADARADA
RADARADARADARADARADARADAR
ADARADARADARADARADARADARA
DARADARADARADARADARADARAD
ARADARADARADARADARADARADA
RADARADARADARADARADARADAR
```

A
AA
ACA
ABCA
ABACA
ABACRA
ABACARA
ABACABRA
ABRACABRA
ABRACDABRA
ABRACADABRA

Richard Kostelanetz, "Abracadabra" from *Illuminations*, 1977

visual poems (*Numbers: Poems & Stories*, 1974), make his self-por-
trait, or write his literary autobiography without any punctua-
tion (*Recyclings: A Literary Autobiography Volume One 1959–67*,
1974). His visual poetry, which resonates strongly with Concrete
Poetry, is fuelled by proliferations, combinations, rotations,
inversions, confrontations, and juxtapositions, compiled by
Kostelanetz in an extensive anthology encompassing many art-
ists and poets (*Imaged Words & Worded Images*, 1970).

FERDINAND KRIWET||||||

From the 1960s onwards, the self-taught German artist Ferdinand Kriwet (1942–2018) sought to bring experimental poetry into the three-dimensional space of the museum, the gallery, and the public space, using films, paintings, books, installations, and a wide variety of performances.

His poetic oeuvre unfolds mainly through two types of forms: the *Sehtexte* (visual texts) are circular compositions whose content appears to be meaningless. In fact, it is impossible for the poet to entirely remove semantics, therefore *Sehtexte* must be seen as open forms. Without beginning nor end, their composition invites the reader to actively participate in their meaning-making.

On the other hand, The *Publit* (contraction of *Public Literature*) aimed to bring poetry into space. Indeed, Kriwet was aware of the new types of language's attentiveness generated by the massive media development and the consumer society's overwhelming stimulation. Similarly, Kriwet played with the advertising's graphic effectiveness (its bold colours, its monumentality) to achieve a literature immediately and simultaneously perceivable by a group of individuals (unlike a book, intended for a solitary reader). Although he has exhibited some of his *Publit* in galleries as paintings, he never considered himself a painter, but rather a writer who used language for its "image value" as well as its "word value". This willingness to decompartmentalize poetry would later inspire him to develop audiovisual environments as well as works for the theater.

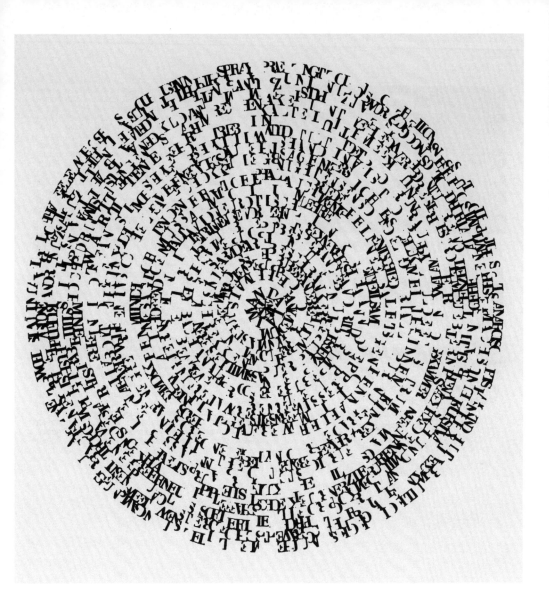

Ferdinand Kriwet, *Rundscheibe nr. XIV*, 1963

Probe
Subway
Tieup
by IAY LEWIS

Target Comes Into Sight

M-DAY MINUS 1

COMPLETE SPORTS | NEW YORK, SATURDAY, JULY 19, 1969 | 15 Cents

FINAL
LATE NEWS
★★★

New York Post

WEATHER
Cloudy,
Chance of
showers,
Saturday, 80s

16-PAGE MAGAZINE • ENTERTAINMENT SECTION • TV 3 RADIO

Who Go | WHAT IT COULD MEAN | Who Wait
The Men | Arnold Toynbee: | The Wives

Journey to the Moon

WEEKEND EDITION

SAT. 1

ROGER ROGER ROGER ROGER ROGER ROGER ROGER ROGER
ROGER ROGER ROGER ROGER ROGER ROGER ROGER ROGER
ROGER ROGER ROGER ROGER ROGER ROGER ROGER ROGER
ROGER ROGER ROGER ROGER ROGER ROGER ROGER ROGER
ROGER ROGER ROGER ROGER ROGER ROGER ROGER ROGER
ROGER ROGER ROGER ROGER ROGER ROGER ROGER ROGER
ROGER ROGER ROGER ROGER ROGER ROGER ROGER ROGER
ROGER ROGER ROGER ROGER ROGER ROGER ROGER ROGER
ROGER ROGER ROGER ROGER ROGER ROGER ROGER ROGER
ROGER ROGER ROGER ROGER ROGER ROGER ROGER ROGER
ROGER ROGER ROGER ROGER ROGER ROGER ROGER ROGER
ROGER ROGER ROGER ROGER ROGER ROGER ROGER ROGER
ROGER ROGER ROGER ROGER ROGER ROGER ROGER ROGER
ROGER ROGER ROGER ROGER ROGER ROGER ROGER ROGER
ROGER ROGER ROGER ROGER ROGER ROGER ROGER ROGER
ROGER ROGER ROGER ROGER ROGER ROGER ROGER ROGER
ROGER ROGER ROGER ROGER ROGER ROGER ROGER ROGER
ROGER ROGER ROGER ROGER ROGER ROGER ROGER ROGER
ROGER ROGER ROGER ROGER ROGER ROGER ROGER ROGER
ROGER ROGER ROGER ROGER ROGER ROGER ROGER ROGER
ROGER ROGER ROGER ROGER ROGER ROGER ROGER ROGER
ROGER ROGER ROGER ROGER ROGER ROGER ROGER ROGER
ROGER ROGER ROGER ROGER ROGER ROGER ROGER ROGER
ROGER ROGER ROGER ROGER ROGER ROGER ROGER ROGER
ROGER ROGER ROGER ROGER ROGER ROGER ROGER ROGER
ROGER ROGER ROGER ROGER ROGER ROGER ROGER ROGER
ROGER ROGER ROGER ROGER ROGER ROGER ROGER ROGER
ROGER ROGER ROGER ROGER ROGER ROGER ROGER ROGER
ROGER ROGER ROGER ROGER ROGER ROGER ROGER ROGER
ROGER ROGER ROGER ROGER ROGER ROGER ROGER ROGER
ROGER ROGER ROGER ROGER ROGER ROGER ROGER ROGER
ROGER ROGER ROGER ROGER ROGER ROGER ROGER ROGER
ROGER ROGER ROGER ROGER ROGER ROGER ROGER ROGER

Although the *Publit* were breaking away from the book space, Kriwet did not necessarily abandon its format. MAMCO acquired *Apollo Amerika* (1969): a book conceived by the German poet while in America, documented the 8 days, 3 hours, 18 minutes, and 35 seconds of the Apollo 11 lunar mission in 1969. Lavishly illustrated, it is a daily journal of texts, newspaper articles, travel forms, photographs, sound recordings, advertisements, illustrations, diagrams, concrete poems, collages, radio broadcasts and television footage, all related to Project Apollo. The historical event's deconstruction across multiple media and mediums has become the poem.

FRANZ MON|||

Franz Mon (*1926) is one of the pioneers of experimental litera-
ture and art breaking new ground in the mid-twentieth century.
His poetic work started in the wake of the go-ahead-spirit that
pervaded all the arts in the 1950s and shattered the boundaries
of genres. The period saw progressive, inter-disciplinary and
cross-media art forms establish a new esthetic of unconventional
means of expression: poetic, typographic, visual, and auditory.

Mon recalled in his memoir *"Wie was begann"* [*How some-
thing started*] what it was that drove those early works: "Art and
literature, hand in hand with the rediscovery and evaluation of
predecessors from the 1920s." One of the key focuses of this
rediscovery was Dada, especially Kurt Schwitters, and the
Surrealists Guillaume Apollinaire and André Breton.

Belonging to the Concrete Poetry movement, he also con-
sidered the question of how few written characters (fragments)
are needed to create some kind of text. For this purpose, any-
thing that resembles a character is good. His raw material con-
sistently includes the daily language of printed mass media.
Overall, his forms of expression can be divided into three strands:
experimental poetry, collages, and radio plays.

In 2020, The exhibition-homage held at MAMCO, whose
title, *Traces of articulation*, refers to Mon's debut volume *"arti-
kulationen"* [*Articulations*, 1959], included examples of all three.
Examples of works using text and language as a material, collages
of visual poetry, and, on the center of the wall, the alphabet poem
"ainmal nur das alphabet gebrauchen" (1967) [*using every letter of*

Franz Mon, *Augen Genau*, 1986

Franz Mon, *Abstrakt*, 1967

the alphabet only one time], a key work in the transition between poetry and visual art, where Mon reshapes and reforms the legibility and comprehensibility of concrete characters imbued with meaning until they become an abstract figure, were thus gathered in the exhibition.

MAURIZIO NANNUCCI

Maurizio Nannucci's (*1939) presence at MAMCO far exceeds the Cabinet of Concrete Poetry. Indeed, four of his text-based neon works have been displayed permanently in the museum's staircase since the institution opened in 1994. Visible on each floor, they juxtapose four words' letters, each in a different color It is therefore the viewer's task to identify these letters, arrange them and eventually decipher "Art," "Text," "Light," and "Sign"—a quartet revealing Nannucci's early artistic program. Since 1967, Nannucci has been working with language using neon lights of various colours. Although the American artist Dan Flavin seized this technology as early as 1963, the Italian was the first to use it scripturally.

Nannucci's earliest linguistic experiments, however, date back to 1963. At that time, he produced typescripts with an Olivetti 22 typewriter. The same word, or even the same letter, is repeated on A4 sheets of variable colors, forming pure geometric patterns. These works foreshadowed the artist's constant search to obliterate any subjective dimension in favor of the graphic and chromatic writing's qualities. Words reclaim their power as symbols, as drawings. A few of these typescripts have been published by Emmet Williams in his first anthology of Concrete Poetry.

Subsequently, this language-based work has multiplied its mediums and devices: postcards, posters, artists' books, anthologies, magazines, stickers, rubber stamps, prints, shopping bags, badges, videos, records, and CDs. So many means for the artist to further explore the public dissemination of the sign. A clock

Maurizio Nannucci, *Art*, 1994

Maurizio Nannucci, *Light*, 1994

made by Nannucci can also be seen on the MAMCO's third floor: the dial's twelve digits have been substituted by twelve letters that make up the expression *quasi infinito* (almost infinite). As we read the time, we also read a text conveying the endless quality of time's unfolding (unless this phrase suggests an inexhaustible relationship between text and image): another way of bringing together the visible and the legible. His illuminated installations also led him to work directly with architecture and public space, he has worked with the architects Renzo Piano, Massimiliano Fuksas, and Mario Botta.

Throughout his career, Nannucci has been involved in numerous collective and experimental projects at the crossroads of Concrete and sound poetry, Conceptual art and the Fluxus movement. In 1968, he founded Exempla, a publishing house still active today, soon followed by Recorthings, an electronic music label. Together with other artists, he initiated independent exhibition spaces in Florence (Zona and then Base) and organized numerous events, actively participating in the local scene. As his artistic networks grew, Nannucci also began collecting materials and documents of all kinds (Mail art, artists' books, posters, photographs, journals, records, etc.), which today comprise the exceptional Zona Archives, showcased from 2017 to 2020 in MAMCO's Cabinet of Concrete Poetry.

RUTH WOLF-REHFELDT

Mail art works by Ruth Wolf-Rehfeldt (b. 1932) have gone around the world, sent as postcards from her home in Berlin—at the time the capital of East Germany—to Western Europe, the Eastern bloc, North America, Latin America, Asia, and New Caledonia.

Created without rules or limitations—except for their format and the cost to mail them—these works of art, freely sent out to like-minded participants, escaped the tyranny of both censors and the art market. In this way, her *Kunstpostbriefe* (art letters) served as independent exhibition spaces, as a means for dialogue and personal correspondence. Wolf-Rehfeldt began working with letters in the early 1970s, creating a series of "type-writings" that combine artistic rigor with a subversive sense of humor. Under her touch, a typewriter's black and red symbols become patterns, butterflies, waves, abstract compositions, and flow charts.

In 2021, MAMCO presented *The Mail Art Archive of Ruth Wolf-Rehfeldt*: an installation that recreates her exchange of correspondence that took place in the 1970s and 1980s. The work was a tribute to the artist's international network of correspondents that she developed over the years via her involvement in the Mail art movement. A slide show, *Mail Art Collaborations*, presented images of collaborative pieces that she worked on at the end of the 1980s. For an exhibition in Norway, Ruth Wolf-Rehfeldt asked several fellow artists to add to her postcards and send them back. This series includes 51 separate works.

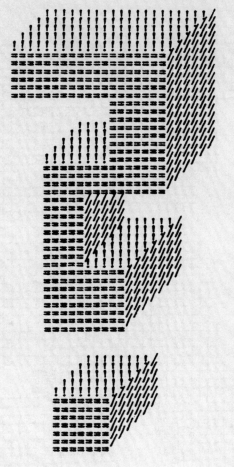

Artitecture 10

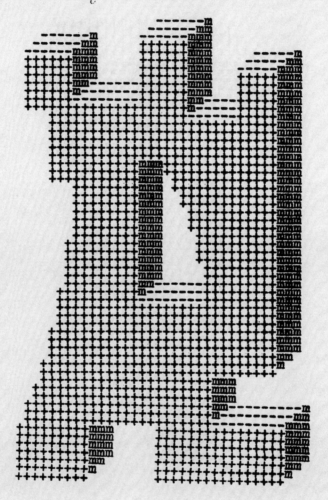

Ruth Wolf-Rehfeldt, *Concrete Figure*, 1979

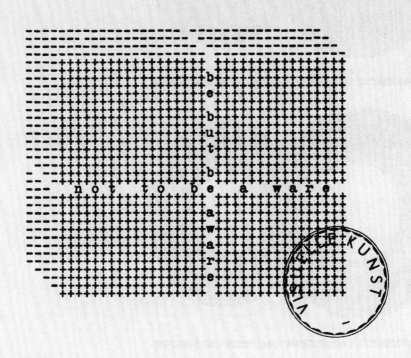

Concrete Advice

WR78

Ruth Wolf-Rehfeldt, *Concrete Advice*, 1978

CONCRETE POETRY AT MAMCO

EXHIBITIONS CATALOGUES AND ANTHOLOGIES

Jasia Reichardt (ed.), *BETWEEN POETRY AND PAINTING*, London: Institute of Contemporary Arts, 1965.

ARLINGTON – UNE, Gloucestershire: Arlington Mill, 1966.

QUADLOG, Dorset: South Street Publications, 1968.

Emmett Williams (ed.), *An of Concrete Poetry*, New York/Villefranche/Francfort: Something Else Press, 1967.

Josef Hirsal and Bohumila Grögerová (eds.), *EXPERIMENTÁLNÍ POEZIE*, Prague: Odeon, 1967.

Eugene Wildman (ed.), *THE CHICAGO REVIEW of concretism*, Chicago: The Swallow Press, 1967.

Form 4. Brighton Festival Exhibition of Concrete Poetry: Notes, Map, Cambridge: Philip Steadman, 1967.

publikaties van de en werk van / publikationen der und arbeiten von / publications by and works by edition hansjörg mayer, The Hague: Haags Gemeentemuseum, 1968.

Jerry G. Bowles et Tony Russell (eds.), *This Book is a Movie. An Exhibition of Language Art and Visual Poetry*, New York: Dell Publishing Co., 1971.

Mary Ellen Solt (ed.), *CONCRETE POETRY: A WORLD VIEW*, Bloomington/London: Indiana University Press, 1970.

Richard Kostelanetz (ed.), *IMAGED WORDS & WORDED IMAGES*, New York: Outerbridge & Dienstfrey, 1970.

J. Laughlin (ed.), *New Directions 22*, New York: New Directions, 1970.

klankteksten konkrete poëzie visuele teksten. sound texts concrete poetry visual texts. akustische texte konkrete poesie visuelle texte, Amsterdam: Stedelijk Museum, 1971.

Peter Finch (ed.), *Typewriter Poems*, New York/Cardiff: Something Else Press/Second Aeon Publications, 1972.

Richard Kostelanetz (ed.), *BREAKTHROUGH FICTIONEERS. An Anthology*, Barton/Brownington/Berlin: Something Else Press, 1973.

ITALIAN VISUAL POETRY. 1912 – 1972, New York: Finch College Museum/Istituto Italiano di Cultura, 1973.

Bob Cobbing (ed.), *GLOUP and WOUP*, Gillingham: Arc Publications, 1974.

TEXT SOUND IMAGE – SMALL PRESS FESTIVAL – 1976, Antwerp: Guy and Anne Schraenen, 1976.

Liselotte Gumpel, *"CONCRETE" POETRY FROM EAST AND WEST. The Language of Exemplarism and Experimentalism*, New Haven/London: Yale University Press, 1976.

Michael Gibbs (ed.), *KONTEXTSOUND*, Amsterdam: Kontexts Publications, 1977.

Bob Cobbing et Peter Mayer (eds.), *concerning concrete poetry*, London: Writers Forum, 1978.

Steve McCaffery and bpNichol (eds.), *SOUND POETRY. A CATALOGUE. For the Eleventh International Sound Poetry Festival,* Toronto: Underwhich Editions, 1978.

LA POESIA VISIVA (1963 – 1979), Florenc: Vallecchi, 1979.

Steven Leiber (ed.), *Ruth and Marvin Sackner Archive of Concrete and Visual Poetry February 1980,* Miami: auto-edition, 1980.

David W. Seaman, *Concrete Poetry in France,* Ann Arbor: UMI Research Press, 1981.

Steven Leiber (ed.), *Ruth and Marvin Sackner Archive of Concrete and Visual Poetry,* Miami: auto-edition, 1986.

Michael Glasmeier, *buchstäblich wörtlich wörtlich buchstäblich,* Berlin: Nationalgalerie Staatliche Museen Preußischer Kulurbesitz, 1987.

LA VIE DES LETTRES. FRENCH ART FROM THE SACKNER ARCHIVE OF CONCRETE AND VISUAL POETRY, Miami: Bass Museum of Art, 1987.

Henri Veyrier (ed.), *POESIA VISIVA. 1963 – 1988. 5 MAESTRI. UGO CARREGA. STELIO MARIA MARTINI. EUGENIO MICCINI. LAMBERTO PIGNOTTI. SARENCO,* Verona: Edizioni Cooperativa "La Favorita", 1988.

Marvin Sackner, *THE ALTERED PAGE. Selections from THE RUTH and MARVIN SACKNER ARCHIVE of CONCRETE and VISUAL POETRY,* New York: Book Arts Gallery, 1988.

Clive Phillpot, *TWENTY YEARS OF BRITISH ART. FROM THE SACKNER ARCHIVE OF CONCRETE AND VISUAL POETRY,* Miami: Bass Museum of Art, 1988.

VII Festival internazionale di poesia, musica, video, performance, danza e teatro, Milan: Ansaldo, 1989.

VISUAL POETRY, Verona/Los Angeles: Rara International/Parsons Gallery, 1990.

The Beauty in Breathing. Selections from The Ruth and Marvin Sackner Archive of Concrete and Visual Poetry, Miami: American Lung Association/ American Thoracis Soecity International Conference, 1992.

Poésure et Peintrie. "d'un art, l'autre.", Marseille : Musées de Marseille, 1993.

die wiener gruppe. the vienna group. a moment of modernity 1954 – 1960 / the visual works and the actions, New York/Vienna: Springer, 1997.

MAGAZINES

AGENTZIA (Paris)
eds. Jochen Gerz
and Jean-François Bory
n° 1 and n° 2 (1967–1968), n° 11/12 (1969)

ANA ECCETERA (Gênes)
ed. Martino Oberto
n° 1 to 8 (1959–1969)

APPROCHES (Paris)
eds. Jean-Francois Bory
and Julien Blaine
n° 1 and n° 2 (1966), n° 4 (1969)

DIAGONAL CERO (La Plata)
ed. Edgardo Antonio Vigo
n° 21 to 24 (1967), n° 26 to 28 (1968)

FUTURA (Stuttgart)
ed. Hansjörg Mayer
n° 1 to 6 (1965–1966), n° 15 and n° 16,
n° 18 to n° 20 (1967), n° 22
to n° 25 (1967–1968)

GEIGER (Turin)
ed. Maurizio Spatola
n° 1 to n° 5 (1967–1972)

GRONK (Vancouver)
ed. bpNichol
n° 2, n° 4, n° 8 (1967)

L'HUMIDITE (Paris)
ed. Jean-François Bory
n° 18 (1973)

INVENÇAO (São Paulo)
ed. Decio Pignatari
n° 4 and n° 5 (1964–1967)

KONTEXTS (Amsterdam)
ed. Michael Gibbs
n° 6, n° 8, n° 9/10 (1975–1977)

LES LETTRES (Paris)
eds. Pierre et Ilse Garnier
n° 29 (1963), n° 34 and n° 35 (1965–1967)

LINEA SUD (Naples)
ed. Luigi Castellano
nᵘ 5 and n° 6 (1967)

LINES (New York)
ed. Aram Saroyan
n° 4 (1965)

MÈLA (Florence)
ed. Maurizio Nannucci
n° 1 to 5 (1976–1981)

NOIGANDRES

POESIA EXPERIMENTAL (Lisbonne)
eds. António Aragão, E.M. de Melo
e Castro, Herberto Helder
n° 2 (1966)

REVUE INTEGRATION (Arnhem)
ed. Herman de Vries
n° 4 (1967)

ROT (Stuttgart)
ed. Hansjörg Mayer
n° 22, n° 24, n° 26, n° 40 (1965–1969)

SERIELLE MANIFESTE 66 (St. Gallen)
ed. Galerie Press
n° I, n° III, n° VII (1966)

SVEP MAGAZINE (Plovdiv, Bulgarie)
ed. Vesselin Sariev
n° 1–4 (1990–1991)

TLALOC (Leeds)
ed. Cavan McCarthy
n° 10 (1966)

WEST COAST POETRY REVIEW
(Reno, USA)
ed. William L. Fox
n° 12–14 (1974)

VERS UNIVERS (Rotterdam)
ed. Frans Vanderlinde
n° 2 to n° 6 (1966–1967)

ARTISTS AND POETS
BELONGING TO THE
CONCRETE POETRY
FUND AT MAMCO

Alain Arias-Misson
Konrad Balder Schäuffelen
Max Bense
Julien Blaine
Jean-François Bory
Vladimir Burda
Klaus Burkhardt
Carlfriedrich Claus
José Luis Castillejo
Henri Chopin
Bob Cobbing
Robin Crozier
Natalie Czech
Augusto de Campos
Haroldo de Campos
Ernesto Manuel Geraldes
    de Melo e Castro
Paul de Vree
Herman de Vries
Klaus Peter Dencker
Wally Depew
Vanessa Deriaz
Mario Diacono
Reinhard Döhl
Luigi Ferro
Peter Finch
Ian Hamilton Finlay
John Furnival
Heinz Gappmayr

Pierre & Ilse Garnier
Jochen Gerz
Mathias Goeritz
Eugen Gomringer
Bohumila Grögerová
José Lino Grünewald
Dom Sylvester Houédard
Hiro Kamimura
Jiří Kolář
Richard Kostelanetz
Ferdinand Kriwet
Arrigo Lora Totino
Hansjörg Mayer
Jean-Claude Moineau
Franz Mon
Edwin Morgan
Tony Morgan
Carsten Nicolai
Seiichi Niikuni
Arthur Pétronio
Claude Rogère
Vesselin Sariev
Aram Saroyan
Peter Schmidt
Adriano Spatola
André Thomkins
Trix + Robert Haussmann
Timm Ulrichs
Jiří Valoch
Wolf Vostell
Lawrence Weiner
Jonathan Williams
Ruth Wolf-Rehfeldt
Louis Zukofsky

Imprint

Editorial Direction
Lionel Bovier

Editorial Coordination
and Redaction
Thierry Davila

Translation
Gauthier Lesturgie

Proofreading
Thierry Davila
Ambroise Tièche

Texts
Paul Bernard
Thierry Davila (Blaine, Bory,
Kostelanetz)

Design
Gavillet & Cie/Devaud

Typefaces
Apax, Practice (www.optimo.ch)

Cover Image
Ruth Wolf-Rehfeldt, *Artitektura, n.d.*
courtesy Chert Lüdde, Berlin

Production
Musumeci S.p.A.
Quart (Aosta)
Italy

Printed and bound in Europe

Published with
ARTBOOKID.A.P.
75 Brood Street
Suite 630
New York
NY 10004
www.artbook.com

ISBN 9781636810423

Crédits photographies
→ Annik Wetter
→ All works reproduced:
collection MAMCO Geneva

Acknowledgements
The MAMCO thanks Maurizio
Nannucci and Gabriele Detterer
for their generous involvement
in this project since its beginning.

The series "MAMCO Collection"
is realized thanks to the support
of the Leenaards Foundation

FONDATION
LEENAARDS

MAMCO
GENEVE

10 rue des Vieux-Grenadiers
CH–1205 Geneva
T +41 22 320 61 22
F + 41 22 781 56 81
E info@mamco.ch

MAMCO opened in 1994 thanks to the perseverance of AMAM (Association for a Modern Art Museum, now Friends of MAMCO) and the generosity of eight patrons, who created the FONDATION MAMCO. Pooling together the support of its Founders and, later, its Co-founders, the foundation was the main source of funding and the sole governing body of the museum up until 2005, when it joined forces with the State and City of Geneva to create a public foundation, known as FONDAMCO.

MAMCO is overseen by FONDAMCO, which is made up of FONDATION MAMCO, the Canton, and City of Geneva. FONDAMCO would like to thank all its partners, both public and private, and in particular: JTI, Fondation Leenaards, and Fondation Valeria Rossi di Montelera, as well as Fondation de bienfaisance du Groupe Pictet, Fondation Bru, Fondation Coromandel, Fondation Lombard Odier, Lenz & Stählin, Mirabaud & Cie SA, Christie's, and Sotheby's.

FONDAMCO

Philippe Bertherat, President
Ronald Asmar, Vice President
Carine Bachmann
Michèle Freiburghaus-Lens
Patrick Fuchs
Jean-Pierre Greff
Jérôme Massard
Marc-André Renold
Simon Studer

FONDATION MAMCO

Council
  Philippe Bertherat, President
  Pierre de Labouchere, Vice President
  Jean Marc Annicchiarico, Treasurer
  Karma Liess-Shakarchi, Secretary
  Charle Beer
  Simon Studer

Founders
  Claude Barbey
  Jean-Paul Croisier
  Pierre Darier
  André L'Huillier
  Philippe Nordmann
  Pierre Mirabaud
  Bernard Sabrier
  —as well as the Friends Association, represented by its President, Patrick Fuchs

Co-founders
  Anne-Shelton et Jean-Michel Aaron
  Tonie and Philippe Bertherat
  Marc Blondeau
  Maryse Bory
  Nicole Ghez de Castelnuovo
  Bénédict Hentsch
  Christina and Pierre de Labouchere
  Aimery Langlois-Meurinne
  Jean-Léonard de Meuron
  Nadine and Edmond de Rothschild
  Lily and Edmond Safra

Patrons
  Afshan Almassi Sturzda
  Jean Marc Annicchiarico
  Tonie and Philippe Bertherat
  Verena and Rémy Best
  Marc Blondeau
  Maryse Bory
  Jean-Paul Croisier
  Darier Family
  Zaza and Philippe Jabre
  Christina and Pierre de Labouchere
  Karma Liess-Shakarchi
  Emmanuelle Maillard
  Jean-Léonard de Meuron
  Patricia and Jean-Pierre Michaux
  Pierre Mirabaud
  Jacqueline and Philippe Nordmann
  Alain-Dominique Perrin
  Marine and Claude Robert
  Bernard Sabrier
  Lily Safra, represented by Samuel Elia
  Simon Studer

TEAM

Lionel Bovier, Director

Museum Management and Development
  Nicole Boissonnas, Public Relations and Development
  Chloë Gouédard, Library, Archives, and Museum Ressources
  Julien Gremaud, Digital Communication
  Viviane Reybier, Press and Communication

Exhibitions and Collection
  Julien Fronsacq, Chief Curator
  Françoise Ninghetto, Honorary Curator
  Sophie Costes, Collection Curator
  Paul Bernard, Curator
  Fabrice Stroun, Associate Curator
  Cyrille Maillot, Chief Exhibition Productions
  Filipe Dos Santos, Exhibition Productions and Collection Registrar
  Pierre-Antoine Héritier and Caroline Dick, Associate Restorers
  Annik Wetter, Associate Photographer

Public and Education Services
  Yann Abrecht, Public Services Manager
  Mathilde Acevedo, Public Services Coordinator
  Daniel Maury, Public Services Coordinator
  Charlotte Morel, Education Services Manager
  Julie Cudet, Education Services Coordinator
  Thierry Davila, Curator in Charge of Publications

Facility Management and Surveillance
  Antonio Magalhes, Chief of Facility Management
  Maria de Fatima Braganca, Facility Management
  Joana Gomes Da Silva, Facility Management
  Carlos Martins Fonseca, Surveillance
  Luc Schuwey, Surveillance